Henry Armitt Brown

Oration of Henry Armitt Brown

On the one hundredth anniversary of the meeting of Congress in

Carpenters' Hall and proceedings in connection therewith

Henry Armitt Brown

Oration of Henry Armitt Brown
*On the one hundredth anniversary of the meeting of Congress in Carpenters' Hall
and proceedings in connection therewith*

ISBN/EAN: 9783337373719

Printed in Europe, USA, Canada, Australia, Japan

Cover: Foto ©ninafisch / pixelio.de

More available books at **www.hansebooks.com**

ORATION

OF

HENRY ARMITT BROWN,

ON THE

ONE HUNDREDTH ANNIVERSARY

OF THE

CARPENTERS' HALL.

MEETING OF CONGRESS IN CARPENTERS' HALL,

AND PROCEEDINGS IN CONNECTION THEREWITH.

PRINTED BY ORDER OF

THE CARPENTERS' COMPANY OF THE CITY AND
COUNTY OF PHILADELPHIA.

1874.

WESTCOTT & THOMSON, .
Stereotypers and Electrotypers, Phila.

TAYLOR & SMITH,
Printers, Phila.

BEAUTIFUL REMINISCENCE

OF THE

FIRST CONGRESS IN PHILADELPHIA.

FROM THE PEN OF THE VENERABLE JOHN ADAMS.

WHEN the Congress met, Mr. Cushing made a motion that it should be opened with prayer. It was opposed by Mr. Jay of New York, and Mr. Rutledge of South Carolina, because we were so divided in religious sentiments—some Episcopalians, some Quakers, some Anabaptists, some Presbyterians, and some Congregationalists—that we could not join in the same act of worship. Mr. Samuel Adams arose and said " that he was no bigot, and could hear a prayer from any gentleman of piety and virtue, who was at the same time a friend to his country. He was a stranger in Philadelphia, but had heard that Mr. Duché (*Duchay* they pronounced it) deserved that character, and therefore he moved that Mr. Duché, an Episcopalian clergyman, might be desired to read prayers to Congress to-morrow morning." The motion was seconded, and passed in the affirmative. Mr. Randolph, our President, waited on Mr. D., and received for answer that if his health would permit he certainly would. Accordingly, next morning he appeared with his clerk and in his pontificals, and read several prayers in the established form, and then read the Psalter for the seventh day of September, which was the thirty-fifth Psalm. You must remember that this was the next morning after we had heard of the horri-

3

ble cannonade of Boston. It seemed as if heaven had ordained that Psalm to be read on that morning.

"After this, Mr. Duché, unexpectedly to everybody, struck out into extemporary prayer, which filled the bosom of every man present. I must confess I never heard a better prayer, or one so well pronounced. Episcopalian as he is, Dr. Cooper himself never prayed with such fervor, such ardor, such correctness and pathos, and in language so elegant and sublime, for America, for Congress, for the Province of the Massachusetts Bay, especially the town of Boston. It had excellent effect upon everybody here. I must beg of you to read the Psalm. If there is any faith in the *sortes Virgilianæ*, or *Homericæ*, or especially the *sortes Biblicæ*, it would have been thought providential."

Here was a scene worthy of the painter's art. It was in Carpenters' Hall in Philadelphia—a building which still survives—that the devoted individuals met to whom this service was read.

Washington was kneeling there, and Henry, and Randolph, and Rutledge, and Lee, and Jay, and by their side there stood, bowed in reverence, the Puritan patriots of New England, who at that moment had reason to believe that an armed soldiery was wasting their humble households. It was believed that Boston had been bombarded and destroyed. They prayed fervently " for America, for the Congress, for the Province of Massachusetts Bay, and especially for the town of Boston," and who can realize the emotions with which they turned imploringly to heaven for divine interposition and aid? "It was enough," says Mr. Adams, "to melt a heart of stone. I saw the tears gush into the eyes of the old, grave, pacific Quakers of Philadelphia."

CARPENTERS' HALL.

At a meeting of "The Carpenters' Company of the City and County of Philadelphia," held 21st of July, 1873,

Resolved, That Walter Allison, D. Henry Flukwir and Richard K. Betts be appointed a committee to memorialize Congress to celebrate the Centennial Meeting of the First Congress in this Hall on September 5, 1874.

October 20, 1874, the Committee presented the draft of a Memorial, which was read and ordered to be transcribed, signed by the President and Secretary, the seal of the Company attached, and the Committee directed to present a copy to the President of the United States and to both Houses of Congress.

MEMORIAL.

To the Senate and House of Representatives of the United States, in Congress assembled:

We, your memorialists, respectfully represent, that, whilst we recognize the fact that our nation's freedom was declared in Independence Hall, yet this Hall, where were heard the deliberate tones of a Hancock, the defiant voice of a Henry, and the persuasive eloquence of an Adams in the First American Congress

—than whom a body of greater men never assembled together or crowned a nation's annals—and who bowed here in reverence as the first prayer was uttered in that Congress, deliberately avowing that to the oppressive acts of the mother-country Americans never can submit, and the determination to part with their liberties only with their lives, so patriotically and faithfully adhered to, is held sacred by us as the Nation's birth-place, and must be dear to every patriotic heart; *and whereas,* The near approach of the one hundredth anniversary of that memorable event renders it befitting that we, the successors of those who freely offered this Hall when even our time-honored State-House was closed against them, should commemorate the nation's advent by our official action; *Therefore be it Resolved,* That Congress be invited to assemble in this Hall on the fifth day of the ninth month next (1874), the hundredth anniversary of the meeting of the First American Congress, and that such ceremonies take place as they in their wisdom may think best suited to that memorable occasion.

SAMUEL RUIN, President.

WM. T. FORSYTHE, *Secretary.*

WALTER ALLISON,
D. HENRY FLUKWIR, } *Committee.*
RICHARD K. BETTS,

July 20, 1874, the Committee reported that two of their number, Walter Allison and Richard K. Betts, proceeded to Washington and presented the Memorial to the President and to Congress as directed.

Walter Allison offered the following:

Whereas, The Carpenters' Company of the City and County of Philadelphia did present a Memorial to the Congress of the United States, inviting that body to celebrate the one-hundredth anniversary of the meeting of Congress in this Hall on the 5th day of September, 1874, and

Whereas, The Congress of the United States have NOT deemed it expedient to celebrate that event as a national one; therefore, be it

Resolved, That in order to celebrate so important an event in our nation's history, a committee of three be appointed, whose duty it shall be to have an oration delivered in this hall, and any other ceremonies appropriate to the occasion; When, on motion, the preamble and resolution were unanimously adopted, and the following committee appointed:

> JOHN M. OGDEN,
> WALTER ALLISON,
> RICHARD K. BETTS.

The Committee extended a timely and cordial invitation to the President of the United States and his Cabinet, the Vice-President, and to both Houses of Congress, the Chief-Justice, the Governors of the States, and other distinguished officials and private citizens.

Amongst those present were

Hon. Henry Wilson, Vice-President, U. S.,

    "   Jos. R. Hawley, M. C. and President of U. S. Centennial Commission,

Hon. Wm. D. Kelley, M. C.,
  " Leonard Myers, "
  " Saml. J. Randall, "
  " Charles O'Neill, "
  " Eli K. Price,
  " James J. Barclay,
  " Daniel M. Fox,
  " Joseph Allison,
  " Wm. S. Peirce,
  " Jas. Lynd,
  " Joseph R. Chandler, Ex-Minister to Italy,
  " James H. Campbell, Ex-Minister to Sweden,
  " Henry C. Carey,
  " Alex. McClure,
Gen. Robert Patterson,
Maj. John O. James,
Capt. George A. Smith,
Hon. Thomas Cochran, } Centennial
  " John Wanamaker, } Board of Finance,
  " Fredk. Fraley, Secretary Centennial Board of
    Finance,
J. L. Atlee, Lancaster,
Leonard H. Davis, Esq., New Jersey.

The assemblage was then called to order by John M. Ogden, chairman of the Committee of Arrangements. He nominated for President John Welsh, Esq.

On motion of Mr. Walter Allison, Charles S. Ogden, Esq., was then chosen Secretary.

Rev. Dr. Thomas F. Davies, Rector of St. Peter's Church, then delivered the following

PRAYER.

O God, who art the blessed and only Potentate, the King of kings and Lord of lords, the Almighty Ruler of Nations, who as at this time didst inspire and direct the hearts of our fathers to lay the perpetual foundations of peace, liberty and safety, we adore and magnify Thy glorious name for all the great things which Thou hast done for us. The Lord our God be with us as He was with our fathers; let Him not leave us nor forsake us. We render Thee thanks for the goodly heritage which Thou hast given us; for the civil and religious privileges which we enjoy, and for the multiplied manifestations of Thy favor. Grant that we may show forth our thankfulness for these Thy mercies, by living in reverence of Thy Almighty power and dominion, in humble reliance on Thy goodness, and in holy obedience to Thy laws. Preserve, we beseech Thee, to our country the blessings of peace, and secure them to all the people of the earth. We implore Thy blessing on all in authority over us, that they may have grace and wisdom so to discharge their duties as most effectually to promote Thy glory, the interests of true religion and virtue, and the peace, good order and welfare of our nation. Shed the quickening influences of Thy Holy Spirit on all the people of this land. Save us from the guilt of abusing our blessings, lest we provoke Thee in just judgment to visit our offences with a rod and our sins with scourges. And while Thy unmerited goodness, O God of all salvation, leads us to repentance, may we offer ourselves, our souls and bodies, a living sacrifice to Thee, who hast preserved and redeemed us, through Jesus Christ our Lord, who hath taught us to pray unto thee, O Almighty Father, in His prevailing name and words. [The reverend gentleman then closed with the Lord's Prayer and Benediction.]

The Secretary, addressing the Chairman, said that he had been requested by Messrs. Wallace & Keller to present to him in their behalf the gavel which he then handed to him, accompanied with authenticated evidences that it was made from wood used in the construction of Independence Hall, with the assurance that it gave to him great pleasure to be the medium of this presentation. The Chairman, on receiving it, thanked the Secretary, and begged him to express to Messrs. Wallace & Keller his grateful acknowledgment for so valuable a token of their kindness, for the presentation of which they had chosen so fitting a moment as this—the centennial of the first meeting of that Congress whose great work had culminated on the 4th of July, 1776, in the Declaration of Independence in Independence Hall. Having been born under the shadow of the spire of that venerable building, and having often in his cradle been lulled to sleep by the sound of that bell which proclaimed liberty throughout the land, he felt that he could, on looking back through a life now well advanced in years, say that he had ever been true to the principles of which they were the symbols; and should it be in the future— which God forbid!—that he should ever be tempted to waver in his allegiance to them, he trusted that this relic (the gavel which he then uplifted), connected so closely with the scenes among which and by which our nation was brought into being, would so strengthen him as to keep him true both to his country and to himself.

The Secretary then read:

PHILADELPHIA, September 4, 1874.

To the President and Managers of the Carpenters' Company of Philadelphia.

GENTLEMEN: A few years since I became possessed of the original portrait, painted by C. W. Peale, of the Hon. Peyton Randolph, the first President of the First Continental Congress. I purchased it, intending that it should be preserved for our city and country on the occasion of the Celebration of the Centennial of the Declaration of Independence. To-morrow will be the One Hundredth Anniversary of the Meeting of the first Congress of the people of the original States, over which Mr. Randolph so ably presided.

I observe that your Company propose to commemorate the Centennial of the first Meeting of the First Continental Congress with appropriate ceremonies, and I can conceive of no memento that will be more suggestive of the great events that have followed the formation of that Congress, than the original portrait of the distinguished patriot and statesman who presided over their deliberations.

Being in full sympathy with the purposes of your Company and the spirit of your proposed celebration, I take pleasure in presenting to you the portrait, to be

placed among the archives of your Company.   With
sentiments of respect, I am

Very truly yours,
E. C. KNIGHT.

Also the following note from Mr. John A. McAllis-
ter:

" It gives me great pleasure to loan to the 'Carpenters' Society,' for its 'Centennial,' a portrait of the
Rev. Jacob Duché, D. D., Chaplain to the 'Continental Congress.' This portrait was drawn in chalk
by the doctor's brother-in-law, Francis Hopkinson
(one of the signers), about the year 1770.   The late
Mrs. Hall, to whom this portrait belonged before it
came into my possession, told me that she was a
friend and frequent visitor of Parson Duché, and that
she considered this the best likeness she had ever
seen."

Colonel Frank M. Etting, of the Museum department, Independence Hall, presented a *fac-simile* of
the signatures of Congress of 1774 to the first convention of *Union* of the Colonies for presentation.
The signatures were made in the Carpenters' Hall by
every delegate then representing the twelve United
Colonies.

Mr. Welsh, President of the meeting, then said:

GENTLEMEN : Official engagements having prevented
his Excellency, the Governor of the Commonwealth,
from presiding on this interesting occasion, that duty
has been assigned to me.   The honor thus conferred
is most grateful to me.   The Carpenters' Company of

the City and County of Philadelphia has sustained a most useful and a most enviable position among the numerous associations which form an essential part of the strength of our great and growing city. Its origin dates as far back as 1724, only forty-two years after William Penn first landed on the shore of the river Delaware. Composed of men engaged in a most useful occupation ; designed to cultivate and uphold among themselves the highest standard of excellence in their art and in their personal characters; embracing in their purpose that most excellent gift of charity which feeds the hungry, clothes the naked, and makes at one the differences which rise among men, —this venerable Company stands to-day, as it has stood through one hundred and fifty years, in undiminished vigor, ever growing in strength and usefulness with its increasing years. Outside of their organization most, if not all, of its members hold a most important relation to our community. Beyond the practical part they take in the pursuit of their calling, there are no classes of men amongst us who labor more earnestly for the public good. Several of those here to-day enjoy the sincerest respect and regard of their fellow-citizens because of their unselfish devotion in the relief of human suffering and to the elevation of the degraded among their fellowmen. Many of its members have, by their judicious enterprise, contributed largely to the material interests of our city, and to their intelligence as a craft we owe the superiority which the private dwellings of Philadelphia possess in convenience and comfort, in addition to their substantial qualities, over those of most other cities. Of their part in the improvement in our styles of architecture honorable mention should be made, for the purpose of obtaining instruction in the science of architecture is one of the objects named in their act of incorporation ; and in the main our architects are but evolutions from carpenters who have worked at the bench. The practical is the best foundation on which to rest an æsthetic superstructure. Nor have the men who, in the long line of succession, have composed this company ever lacked sympathy with the advancing sentiment of the country. In patriotic feeling their hearts have always beat in unison with the most ardent advocates of liberty. The occasion of our meeting to-day bears the strongest possible testimony on that point. It was in this venerable Hall—venerable alike for its age and its honors —that the First Congress assembled. Here, where we now are, that memorable meeting took place, on this day one hundred years ago. Well might we pause and try to recall that scene, but the attempt to do it is not for me. One mightier far than I am for such a purpose will follow me, and the sketch, with all its circumstances, the actors in it and its consequences, shall be given you by his graphic pencil. Let me, however, ask of you to look for a single moment through the vista of the many intervening years upon the dark background which closes it—dark with the clouds of impending perils, of doubts and fears, of sacrifices and of sufferings, with here and there upon these clouds slight fissures of gilded light, foreshadow-

ing feebly the lofty aims and firm resolves of our forefathers, which, like the faint gleams of hope and
smouldering sparks of future glory nourished within
their bosoms, led them forward; and tell me whether,
in bringing back your vision to the present, the grandeur of our possessions does not startle you with
alarm at your own insensibility as to their extent, and
with the weight of the responsibility resting on you
for the proper use of the material wealth and the civil
and religious privileges in which our country literally
revels—the fruits of the seed planted under such
bitter adversity?

Is not this a thought worthy of our consideration?
Is it not *the* thought which for years past has been
making itself a home in the hearts of many of our
people, taking them back into the past, and filling
them with apprehension for the future, lest, losing
sight of the true elements of our strength, our prosperity should become our weakness? This may well
cause us to look toward 1876 with longings for a re-
union, that we may study anew the principles of our
institutions, and honor those who established them
here on the very spot rendered classic by the scenes
incident to the mighty transformation wrought in 1776,
by which thirteen colonies, subject to the kingdom of
Great Britain and Ireland, became an independent
nation, based on the principle of self-government,
known ever since as "the United States of America,"
and now respected as one among the great powers of
the earth. It is that longing hope, common, as I believe, to every one who claims our flag as his protec-

tion, which has been crystallized into a reality by Congress in the act of 3d March, 1871. That act created a commission, drawn from every State and Territory, to make suitable provision for a Centennial Celebration in the city of Philadelphia in 1876, one of the principal features of which shall be an International Exhibition of the arts and manufactures of other nations, in contrast with those of our own production ; and beyond this, by every suitable means, to recall the events and the actors in those interesting scenes which radiate from that great central light—the Declaration of Independence, the memories of which have become too faint in the minds of the great mass of our people. When we look with pride on the progress we have made in a century; when we count the many millions which now people our great cities and broad plains ; bring in array the fields covered with cotton and the golden grain ; hear the busy sound of machinery reverberating from hill to valley, mingling with the bleating and lowing of flocks and herds innumerable ; descend beneath the surface, where thousands toil for the rich rewards of mineral wealth ; look upon the trains traversing seventy thousand miles of railroad within our borders, extending from ocean to ocean, and making almost every hamlet in the land accessible ; mark on our great rivers and canals vessels of every form in incessant motion ; and see our flag unfurled on every sea and in every harbor,—it is wise that we should recall the events in which our prosperity took its rise, study the principles on which it was based, dwell on the simplicity of the lives and

the purity and strength of the men who brought about
these great results, and make ourselves familiar with
them all, that if, because of our departure from their
principles or their examples, we are the weaker for it,
and are unable to recover ourselves, we may at least
teach them to our children, and thus, through them,
renew the foundation which can alone support so
grand a superstructure.

One of the first fruits of this approaching Centennial is now at hand. This same Carpenters' Company,
which in 1774 opened its hall to the Continental Congress, animated by the same spirit as it was moved by
then, and in view of the celebration to be held in 1876,
has assembled here to-day to revive in the memory of
its countrymen a knowledge of the men who met in
this Hall on the 5th of September, 1774, one hundred
years ago. God grant that in this noble effort they
may be successful!

Gentlemen, I have now the pleasure to introduce to
you HENRY ARMITT BROWN, Esq., who will address you
in furtherance of this patriotic purpose.

HENRY ARMITT BROWN then came forward and read
a letter, which he had just received, from the Hon.
Wm. S. Stokley, Mayor of Philadelphia, desiring him,
as Orator of the Day, to extend an invitation, in His
Honor's name, to the distinguished company present,
to visit Independence Hall and the National Museum
after the exercises in Carpenters' Hall. Having dis-
charged, in a few words, the pleasant duty thus con-
fided to him, he continued as follows.

2

ORATION

HENRY ARMITT BROWN.

WE have come here to-day in obedience to that natural impulse which bids a people do honor to its past. We have assembled to commemorate a great event—one of the most famous in our history. In the midst of prosperity and profound peace; in the presence of the honorable and honored Vice-President of the United States, of the chosen rulers of the people, of the members of the present and other Congresses—the successors of the statesmen of 1774—of the representatives of the learned professions, and of every department of human enterprise and industry and skill, we have gathered beneath this roof to celebrate, with reverent and appropriate services, the one hundredth anniversary of the meeting of the First Continental Congress.

It is a great privilege to be here, and we have to thank the Carpenters' Company for it. The Carpenters' Company of Philadelphia has always been a patriotic body. In the months which preceded the Revolution it freely offered its hall for the meetings of the people; and besides the high honor of having entertained the Congress of 1774, it can point to its having sheltered the Committees of Safety and the Provincial

18

Committee for a long time beneath this roof. The Carpenters' Company of Philadelphia is a very ancient body. It came into existence when George the First was king, when Benjamin Franklin was a printer's lad, and Samuel Johnson was a boy at school. It was founded fifty years before an American Congress met, and it is now half as old again as American independence. And more than this, it is a very honorable body. Its members have been counted among our best citizens for industry and character. Both this hall, in which the nation may be said to have been born, and that other, where in 1776 its articles of apprenticeship were cancelled, are the monuments of its earlier skill, and there are few houses in this City of Homes in which its members have not had a hand. And, after all, how fitting does it seem that the hall of the Carpenters' Company should have been the scene of that event which we have assembled to commemorate! The men of the First Congress were architects themselves; the master-builders of a Republic founded on the equality of man—the highest types of which, in the two struggles through which it has had to pass, have been Benjamin Franklin, the mechanic, and the farmer's lad whose name was Abraham Lincoln. They represented among themselves every rank of life—the lawyer, the merchant, the farmer, the mechanic—and they did more to dignify Labor and advance the cause of Humanity in the seven weeks during which they sat in this place than all the parliaments of the world have done in twice as many centuries. If there be anything good, if there be anything noble, if there be anything precious in the American Revolution, it is just this—that it secured for every man an equal chance. Far wiser than those who have attempted a similar work beneath other skies, the men who achieved that Revolution attacked no vested rights, set up no false notions of equality, nor the oppression of the many for the tyranny of the few, nor did they break the chain that bound them to an honorable past. They sought rather to make Virtue and Intelligence the test of manhood—to strike down Prerogative and Privilege and open the gates of happiness to all alike.   And as I contemplate their glorious struggle at this distance of time, and think of the national life which it has blessed us with—a century of which is surely a great achievement for any people*—I cannot but think it to have been a happy omen that it was inaugurated here. It is impossible, in the time which I can allow myself, to attempt a description of the causes of the Revolu-

---

* The historian Freeman, writing in 1862, says (*Hist. of Fed. Govt.*, vol. i., p. 112): "At all events, the American Union has actually secured, for what is really a long period of time, a greater amount of combined peace and freedom than was ever before enjoyed by so large a portion of the earth's surface. There have been, and still are, vaster despotic empires, but never before has so large an inhabited territory remained for more than seventy years in the enjoyment at once of internal freedom and of exemption from the scourge of internal war."

Prof Hoppin of Yale College tells me of a conversation he had some years ago with Prof. Karl von Raumer of Berlin : " I asked him what was his opinion as to the perpetuity of republican institutions. He said : Under certain conditions fulfilled, they would be more permanent than any other form. ' But,' said he, starting up from his chair with great energy, ' if they should fail, fifty years of American freedom would be worth a thousand years of Siberian despotism !' "

A similar thought is expressed by Freeman in page 52 of the volume above quoted: " The one century of Athenian greatness, from the expulsion of the Thirty Tyrants to the defeat of Aigospotamos, is worth millenniums of the life of Egypt or Assyria."

tion. The duty which I have to discharge is sufficiently difficult. I shall tax your patience, at any rate, I fear, (for the trial is rather how little than how much to say), but the story must needs be long, and the occasion seems one of historic dignity.

It was only a month ago that the inhabitants of a little island in the northern corner of the Atlantic Ocean met on their Law Mount and celebrated, with song and saga, their one thousandth anniversary. That hardy race, which counts among its achievements the first discovery of this continent, has witnessed many memorable and strange events. Locked up in snow and ice, protected by the warring elements, it has watched the growth and decay of empires, the rise and fall of nations, the most wonderful changes in every quarter of the globe. But it has seen no spectacle more extraordinary than that which we commemorate to-day, and in all the sterile pages of its thousand years of history it can point to no such achievements as fill up the first century of this younger nation.

The tendency of the American colonies toward union had frequently shown itself before 1774. There was, of course, little sympathy at the outset between the Puritan of New England and the Virginian cavalier, the Roman Catholic of Maryland and the Pennsylvania Quaker. Each had, in times past, suffered at the other's hands, and the smart of their injuries was not soon forgotten. But time, that great healer, came after a while to efface its sharpness, and when the third generation had grown up little bitterness re-

mained. For, after all, there is no sympathy like that
which is begotten by common suffering. The trials
of these men had been much the same. The spirit of
persecution had driven forth all alike. Their ideas of
liberty—narrow as they were at first—did not mate-
rially differ, and their devotion to them had led all
alike across the seas. They spoke the same language,
inherited the same traditions, revered the same examples, worshipped the same God. Nor had the ob-
stacles which they had overcome been different. Heat
and cold, fire and sword, hunger and thirst—they had
all experienced these. The Frenchman on the North
and the Indian along the Western frontier had constantly threatened them with a common danger, and
when the news of Braddock's defeat came down the
slopes of the Alleghany Mountains it sent a thrill
through hearts in Georgia and New Hampshire, as
well as in Pennsylvania and Maryland. As early as
the year 1754 the Indian troubles and the necessity
for united action had led to the assembling of a convention or council at Albany, at which seven colonies
were represented. The scheme for a perpetual union
which the genius of Franklin had then devised was
not successful, it is true, but the meeting under such
circumstances awakened a strong desire for union
among his countrymen; and when, in 1765, the times
had changed, and the mother-country, victorious over
France, turned her hand against her children, the
sense of danger found expression in the convention
which the Stamp Act brought together in New York.
I pass without comment over the years which inter-

vened between 1765 and 1774. The Stamp Act had been repealed, but a succession of severer measures had brought things from bad to worse. Great Britain was in the zenith of her power. The colonies were thirteen in number, and contained about two millions and a half of inhabitants.* Let us, then, in the course of the hour which we are to spend together here, endeavor to go back in imagination to the summer of 1774. Here in Philadelphia there have been feverish days. The news of the determination of the ministry to shut up the port of Boston, followed as it is soon after by the attempt to do away with the ancient charter of Massachusetts and to remove to Great Britain the trial of offences committed in America, has aroused the patriotic resistance of the whole country. In every town and hamlet, from New Hampshire to the southern boundary of Georgia, bold protests are recorded by the people, and Boston is declared to be suffering in the common cause. The first day of June, when the Port Bill goes into effect, is everywhere kept as a day of fasting and humiliation. Flags are lowered to half-mast, shops shut up and the places of worship crowded with thoughtful men. Nine-tenths of the houses in Philadelphia are closed in mourning, and the famous bells of Christ Church are muffled in distress. Nor are the fellow-countrymen of the Bostonians content with this manifestation of their sympathy. From every part of the colonies come contributions for the suffering poor. Money, provisions and articles of clothing pour in

---

* Bancroft, *Hist. U. S.*, vol. vii., page 128.

from every side. There is but one sentiment in the great majority of the people—a determination to support the men of Massachusetts to the end. They were not unconscious of the dangers of such a course. The disparity between the power of Great Britain and their own was far more apparent to them than it can ever be to us. They saw her the first power of the age—fresh from the memorable wars in which she had destroyed the naval and colonial power of France. The air still rang with the cheers with which they had greeted her successive triumphs, each of which they had come to look upon as their own. Her armies had been victorious in every land, her fleets triumphant on the most distant seas, and whatever of spirit, of courage and of endurance they might believe themselves to possess they had inherited from her. " We have not fit men for the times," wrote one of the leading actors in the drama that was about to begin; "we are deficient in genius, in education, in travel, in fortune, in everything. I feel unutterable anxiety." * But there is no thought of yielding in anybody's breast. " God grant us wisdom and fortitude," writes John Adams, in June, and he speaks the universal sentiment of his countrymen. " Should the opposition be suppressed, should this country submit, what infamy and ruin! God forbid! Death in any form is less terrible."† It was out of this consciousness of weakness that the strength of the Revolution grew. Had Massachusetts stood alone, had a feeling of strength seduced the colonies to remain divided, the end would

---

* *Works of John Adams*, vol. ii., p. 338.   † *Idem.*

have been far different. Singly, they would have offered but a slight resistance—together, they were invincible. And the blind policy of the English king and ministry steadily fostered this sentiment of union. The closing of the port of Boston was intended by its authors to punish Massachusetts alone, but the merchant of Charleston or New York saw in the act the attempt to exercise a power which might one day be directed against him, and the Pennsylvanian could have little feeling of security in submitting his valued institutions to the mercy of those who sought, by an act of Parliament, to sweep away the ancient charter of Massachusetts. The cause of one colony became the cause of all. The rights of Massachusetts were the rights of America.

All through the spring and summer there has been concert and consultation. Couriers are riding here and there with messages from the Committees of Correspondence which, thanks to Samuel Adams, have been established in every village. A constant interchange of counsels has soon begotten confidence; with better understanding has come a sense of strength. Each colony seems ready for her share of the responsibility, and no town, however feeble, feels alone. Boston is strengthened in her glorious martyrdom as her sister towns reach forth to clasp her shackled hands, and the cry goes forth, at last, for the assembling of a Continental Congress. " Permit me to suggest a general Congress of deputies from the several Houses of Assembly on the Continent," * John

* Bancroft's *Hist. U. S.*, vol. vi., p. 508.

Hancock says on the 4th of March, "as the most effectual method of establishing a union for the security of our rights and liberties." "A Congress, and then an Assembly of States,"* cries Samuel Adams, in April, 1773. Here is a call for a general Congress in the newspaper which I hold in my hand —a journal published in Philadelphia on the 11th of October, 1773. "A Congress," suggest the Sons of Liberty of New York in the spring of the following year, and in all parts of the country the cry meets with a response. The first official call comes from Virginia, dated May 28, 1774. On the 20th of that month the Whigs of Philadelphia have met, to the number of three hundred, in the long room of the City Tavern on Second Street, and, after consultation, unanimously resolved that the Governor be asked at once to call a meeting of the Assembly of this Province, and a Committee of Correspondence be appointed to write to the men of Boston "that we consider them as suffering in the general cause;" "that we truly feel for their unhappy situation;" "that we recommend to them firmness, prudence and moderation;" and that "we shall continue to evince our firm adherence to the cause of American liberty." †

* Bancroft's *Hist. U. S.*, vol. vi., p. 456.

† *Pennsylvania Packet*, for June 6, 1774. The reply to the Bostonians was written by the Rev. Dr. Wm. Smith, first Provost of the University of Pennsylvania (who did service afterward as one of the Provincial Convention of 1774). An interesting account of this will be found on pages forty-one and forty-two of the valuable *Memoir of the Rev. William Smith, D. D.;* for a copy of which I am indebted to its author, Charles J. Stillé, Esq., LL.D., the present Provost of the University.

The messenger who bears this letter finds the country all alive. The Boston Committee sends southward a calm statement of the situation, and asks for general counsel and support. Rumor follows rumor as the days go by, and presently a courier comes riding down the dusty king's highway from the North, and never draws rein till he reaches the Merchants' Coffee House, where the patriots are assembled in committee. The intelligence he brings is stirring, for men come forward with flushed cheeks and sparkling eyes. And soon it is on every lip. Behold, great news! Bold Sam Adams has locked the Assembly door on the king's officers at Salem, and the General Court has named Philadelphia and the first of September as the place and time for the assembling of a Congress of Deputies from all the colonies. Twelve hundred miles of coast is soon aflame. Nor is the enthusiasm confined to youth alone. Hopkins and Hawley in New England, and Gadsden in Carolina, are as full of fire as their younger brethren, and far away, in a corner of the British capital, a stout old gentleman in a suit of gray cloth, with spectacles on his nose and a bright twinkle in his eye, is steadily preparing for the struggle which he—wise, far-sighted, great-souled Franklin—has long foreseen and hoped for. One by one the colonies choose delegates. Connecticut first, Massachusetts next, Maryland the third, New Hampshire on the 21st of July, Pennsylvania on the 22d, and so on until all but Georgia have elected representatives. Yet still king and Parliament are deaf and blind, royal governors are writing: " Massachusetts stands

alone; there will be no Congress of the other colonies." Boston lies still, the shipping motionless in her
harbor, the merchandise rotting on her wharves, and
elsewhere, as of old, the dull routine of provincial life
goes jogging on. The creaking stages lumber to and
fro. Ships sail slowly up to town, or swing out into
the stream waiting for a wind to take them out to sea.
Men rise and go to work, eat, lie down and sleep.
The sun looks down on hot, deserted streets, and so
the long days of summer pass until September comes.
With the first days of the new month there is excitement among the Philadelphia Whigs. All through the
week the delegates to Congress have been arriving.
Yesterday, Christopher Gadsden and Thomas Lynch,
Esquires, landed at the wharf, having come by sea
from Charleston, South Carolina; to-day, Colonel Nathaniel Folsom and Major John Sullivan, the delegates
from New Hampshire, ride into town.* The friends
of liberty are busy. The great coach-and-four† of John
Dickinson rolls rapidly through the streets as he has-
tens to greet the Virginian gentlemen who have just
arrived, and in the northern suburbs a company of
horsemen has galloped out the old King's Road to
welcome the delegates from Massachusetts, who have
arrived at Frankford, with Sam Adams at their head.‡

---

* *Pennsylvania Packet*, for Aug. 29, 1774.

† "Mr. Dickinson, the farmer of Pennsylvania, came in his coach, with four
beautiful horses, to Mr. Ward's lodgings to see us."—*J. Adams' Works*, vol.
ii., p. 360.

‡ *Idem*, p. 357, "After dinner we stopped at Frankford, about five miles out
of town. A number of carriages and gentlemen came out of Philadelphia to
meet us. . . . We were introduced to all these gentlemen, and cordially wel-

With Saturday night they are all here, save those from North Carolina, who were not chosen till the 25th, but are on their way.

Sunday comes—the last Sabbath of the old provincial days. The bells of Christ Church chime sweetly in the morning air, and her aisles are crowded beyond their wont; but the solemn service glides along, as in other days, with its prayer for king and queen, so soon to be read for the last time within those walls; and the thought, perhaps, never breaks the stillness of the Quakers' meeting-house that a thing has come to pass that will make their quiet town immortal. Then the long afternoon fades away and the sun sinks down yonder over Valley Forge.

The fifth day of September dawns at last. At ten in the morning the delegates assemble at the Merchants' Coffee House.* From that point they march on foot along the street until they reach the threshold of this hall. And what a memorable procession! The young men cluster around them as they pass, for these are their chosen leaders in the struggle that has come. The women peep at them, wonderingly, from the

comed to Philadelphia. We then rode into the town, and, dirty, dusty and fatigued as we were, we could not resist the importunity to go to the tavern, the most genteel one in America." The important consequences of this meeting at Frankford are set forth in a letter of Adams to T. Pickering in 1822, printed in a note on page 512 of the same volume. *Vide,* also, vol. i., p. 151.

* Then called the City Tavern. It stood on the west side of Second street, above Walnut, at the corner of Gold street (or Bank alley), and had been recently opened by Daniel Smith. It was already the rendezvous of the Whigs, as the London Coffee House (still standing), at Front and Market, had long been of the Tory party.—*Vide* WESTCOTT'S *Hist. of Phila.,* Philadelphia Library copy, vol. ii., p. 364.

bowed windows of their low-roofed houses, little
dreaming, perhaps, that these are the fathers of a
republic for the sake of which their hearts are soon
to be wrung and their homes made desolate.   Here a
royalist—"Tory" he is soon to be called—turns out
for them to pass, scarcely attempting to hide the sneer
that trembles on his lips, or some stern-browed Friend,
a man of peace, his broad-brimmed hat set firmly on
his head, goes by, with measured footsteps, on the
other side.   Yonder urchin, playing by the roadside,
turns his head suddenly to stare at this stately company.   Does he dream of the wonders he shall live
to see?   Men whose names his children shall revere
through all descending generations have brushed by
him while he played, and yet he knows them not.

And so along the street, and down the narrow court,
and up the broad steps the Congress takes its way.
The place of meeting has been well chosen.   Some
of the Pennsylvanians would have preferred the State-
House, but that is the seat of Government, and the
Assembly, which has adjourned, has made no provision for the meeting of Congress there.   Here, too,
have been held the town-meetings at which the people
have protested against the acts of Parliament, and the
Carpenters' Company, which owns the hall, is made
up of the friends of liberty.   It has offered its hall to
the delegates, and the place seems fit.   It is "a spa-
cious hall," says one of them,* and above there is "a
chamber, with an excellent library," "a convenient

---

* John Adams, from whose *Journal* or *Correspondence* I have taken the personal descriptions in nearly every instance.

chamber opposite to this, and a long entry where gentlemen may walk." The question is put whether the gentlemen are satisfied, and passed in the affirmative ; the members are soon seated and the doors are shut. The silence is first broken by Mr. Lynch of South Carolina. " There is a gentleman present," he says, " who has presided with great dignity over a very respectable society, and greatly to the advantage of America ;" and he " moves that the Honorable Peyton Randolph, Esquire, one of the delegates from Virginia, be appointed chairman." He doubts not it will be unanimous. It is so, and yonder,* "large well-looking man," carefully dressed, with well-powdered wig and scarlet coat, rises and takes the chair. The commissions of the delegates are then produced and read, after which Mr. Lynch nominates as secretary Mr. Charles Thomson, "a gentleman," he says, " of family, fortune and character." And thereupon, with that singular wisdom which our early statesmen showed in their selection of men for all posts of responsibility, the Congress calls into his country's service that admirable man, " the Sam Adams of Philadelphia and the life of the cause of liberty." † While the pre-

---

* During the delivery of this address an original portrait of Mr. Randolph hung above the chair in which he sat during the sessions of Congress.

† The Hon. Eli K. Price has kindly sent me the following interesting account of the manner in which this was made known to Mr. Thomson. The allusion in the address " reminded me," writes a lady of Mr. Price's family, Miss Rebecca Embree, " of the great simplicity of that appointment, as I have heard it related by Deborah Logan, wife of Dr. George Logan of Stenton, viz. : ' Charles Thomson had accompanied his wife on a bridal visit to Deborah Logan's mother, Mary Parker Norris, who resided on Chestnut street above Fourth, where the Custom-House now stands. Whilst there a messenger arrived inquiring for Mr.

liminaries are being despatched, let us take a look at this company, for it is the most extraordinary assemblage America has ever seen. There are fifty delegates present, the representatives of eleven colonies. Georgia has had no election, the North Carolinians have not yet arrived, and John Dickinson, that "shadow, slender as a reed, and pale as ashes," that Pennsylvania farmer who has sown the seeds of empire, is not a member yet.[*] Directly in front, in a seat of prominence, sits Richard Henry Lee. His brilliant eye and Roman profile would make him a marked man in any company. One hand has been injured, and is wrapped, as you see, in a covering of black silk, but when he speaks his movements are so graceful and his voice so sweet that you forget the defect of gesture, for he is an orator—the greatest in America, perhaps, save only one. That tall man with the swarthy face and black, unpowdered hair, is

Thomson, and informed him that he was wanted at Carpenters' Hall. Being introduced to the company there assembled, he was requested to act as their secretary, which he accordingly did.' "

[*] Justice is not done now-a-days to the patriotic labors of John Dickinson. The effect of his *Farmer's Letters* in preparing the minds of his countrymen for resistance to Great Britain can hardly be exaggerated, and to him they owed the phrase "No taxation without representation." When the Congress of 1774 assembled no man in the colonies was more prominent than the Farmer, and his influence upon its deliberations was very great. On page 13 of the valuable *Early History of the Falls of Schuylkill, etc. etc.*, by Charles V. Hagner, Esq., will be found an interesting account, taken partly from the *Pennsylvania Gazette* of May 12, 1768, of the presentation of a laudatory address to Mr. Dickinson by the Society of Fort St. Davids. Other similar addresses were sent to him from various parts of the colonies—one especially worthy of note being signed by Dr. Benjamin Church, John Hancock, Samuel Adams, Dr. Joseph Warren, and John Rowe, and enclosing resolutions adopted at a town-meeting held in Boston.

William Livingston of New Jersey—"no public speaker, but sensible and learned." Beside him, with his slender form bent forward and his face lit with enthusiasm, sits his son-in-law, John Jay, soon to be famous. He is the youngest of the delegates, and yonder sits the oldest of them all. His form is bent, his thin locks fringing a forehead bowed with age and honorable service, and his hands shake tremulously as he folds them in his lap. It is Stephen Hopkins, once Chief-Justice of Rhode Island. Close by him is his colleague, Samuel Ward, and Sherman of Connecti-cut—that strong man whose name is to be made honorable by more than one generation. Johnson of Maryland is here, "that clear, cool head," and Paca, his colleague, "a wise deliberator." Bland of Virginia is that learned-looking, "bookish man" beside "zeal-ous, hot-headed" Edward Rutledge. The Pennsyl-vanians are grouped together at one side—Morton, Humphreys, Mifflin, Rhoads, Biddle, Ross, and Gallo-way, the Speaker of the Assembly. Bending forward to whisper in the latter's ear is Duane of New York— that sly-looking man, a little "squint-eyed" (John Adams has already written of him), "very sensible and very artful." That large-featured man, with the broad, open countenance, is William Hooper; that other, with the Roman nose, McKean of Delaware. Rodney, the latter's colleague, sits beside him, "the oddest-looking man in the world—tall, thin, pale, his face no bigger than a large apple, yet beaming with sense, and wit, and humor." Yonder is Christopher Gadsden, who has been preaching independence to

South Carolina these ten years past. He it is who,
roused by the report that the regulars have com-
menced to bombard Boston, proposes to march north-
ward and defeat Gage at once, before his reinforce-
ments can arrive; and when some one timidly says
that in the event of war the British will destroy the
sea-port towns, turns on the speaker, with this grand
reply: "Our towns are built of brick and wood; if
they are burned down we can rebuild them; but liberty once lost is gone for ever." In all this famous
company perhaps the men most noticed are the Massachusetts members. That colony has thus far taken
the lead in the struggle with the mother-country. A
British army is encamped upon her soil; the gates of
her chief town are shut; against her people the full
force of the resentment of king and Parliament is
spent. Her sufferings called this Congress into being,
and now lend sad prominence to her ambassadors.
And of them surely Samuel Adams is the chief.
What must be his emotions as he sits here to-day—
he who "eats little, drinks little, sleeps little, and
thinks much "*—that strong man whose undaunted
spirit has led his countrymen up to the possibilities of
this day? It is his plan of correspondence, adopted,
after a hard struggle, in November, 1772, that first
made feasible a union in the common defence. He
called for union as early as April, 1773. For that he
had labored without ceasing and without end, now
arousing the drooping spirits of less sanguine men,

* *Historical and Political Reflections on the Rise and Progress of the American Rebellion*, by JOSEPH GALLOWAY, London, 1780.

now repressing the enthusiasm of rash hearts, which threatened to bring on a crisis before the time was ripe, and all the while thundering against tyranny through the columns of the Boston *Gazette*. As he was ten years ago he is to-day, the master-spirit of the time—as cool, as watchful, as steadfast, now that the hour of his triumph is at hand, as when, in darker days, he took up the burden James Otis could no longer bear. Beside him sits his younger kinsman, John Adams, a man after his own heart—bold, fertile, resolute, an eloquent speaker and a leader of men. But whose is yonder tall and manly form? It is that of a man of forty years of age, in the prime of vigorous manhood. He has not spoken, for he is no orator, but there is a look of command in his broad face and firm-set mouth that marks him among men, and seems to justify the deference with which his colleagues turn to speak with him. He has taken a back seat, as becomes one of his great modesty—for he is great even in that—but he is still the foremost man in all this company. This is he who has just made in the Virginia Convention that speech which Lynch of Carolina says is the most eloquent speech that ever was made: "I will raise a thousand men, subsist them at my own expense, and march with them at their head for the relief of Boston." These were his words—and his name is Washington. Such was the Continental Congress assembled in Philadelphia.

Its members were met by a serious difficulty at the very outset. The question at once arose, How should their votes be cast—by colonies, by interest, or by the

poll? Some were for a vote by colonies; but the
larger ones at once raised the important objection that
it would be unjust to allow to a little colony the same
weight as a large one. "A small colony," was the
reply of Major Sullivan of New Hampshire, "has its all
at stake, as well as a large one." Virginia, responded
the delegates from the Old Dominion, will never consent to waive her full representation; and one of them
went so far as to intimate that if she were denied an
influence in proportion to her size and numbers, she
would never again be represented in such an assembly. On the other hand, it was confessed to be impossible to determine the relative weight which should
be assigned to each colony. There were no tables of
population, of products, or of trade, nor had there been
a common system in the choice of delegates. Each
province had sent as many as it liked—Massachusetts
four, South Carolina five, Virginia seven, Pennsylvania
eight. In one case they had been chosen by a convention of the people, in another by a general election, in most by the Assembly of the province. There
was no rule by which the members could be guided.
Nor was this the only point of difference among the
delegates. On no one thing did they seem at first
sight to agree. Some were for resting their rights
on a historical basis—others upon the law of nature.
These acknowledged the power of Great Britain to
regulate trade—those denied her right to legislate for
America at all. One would have omitted the Quebec
bill from the list of grievances—another held it to be
of them all the very worst. Some were for paying

an indemnity for the destruction of the tea—others cried out that this were to yield the point at once. One was defiant, a second conciliatory; Gadsden desired independence; Washington believed that it was wished for by no thinking man.

It was with a full sense of the diversity of these views, of the importance of a speedy decision, and of the danger of dissension, that the Congress reassembled the next morning.

When the doors had been closed and the preliminaries gone through with, it is related that an oppressive silence prevailed for a long time before any man spoke. No one seemed willing to take the lead. It was a season of great doubt and greater danger. Now, for the first time perhaps, when the excitement of the assembling had passed away, and reflection had come to calm men's minds, the members realized completely the importance of their acts. Their countrymen watched and waited everywhere. In the most distant hamlet beyond the mountains, in the lonely cabin by the sea, eyes were turned to this place with anxious longing, and yonder, in the North, the brave town lay patient in her chains, resting her hopes for deliverance upon them. And not Boston only, nor Massachusetts, depended upon them. The fate of humanity for generations was to be affected by their acts. Perhaps in the stillness of this morning hour there came to some of them a vision of the time to come. Perhaps to him on whose great heart was destined so long to lie the weight of all America it was permitted to look beyond the present hour, like that great leader of an earlier race when he stood silent upon a peak in Moab and overlooked the Promised Land. Like him, he was to be the chosen of his people. Like him, soldier, lawgiver, statesman. Like him, he was destined to lead his brethren through the wilderness; and, happier than he, was to behold the fulfilment of his labor. Perhaps, as he sat here in the solemn stillness that fell upon this company, he may have seen, in imagination, the wonders of the century that is complete to-day. If he had spoken, might he not have said: I see a winter of trouble and distress, and then the smoke of cannon in the North. I see long years of suffering to be borne, our cities sacked, our fields laid waste, our hearths made desolate; men trudging heavily through blood-stained snow, and wailing women refusing to be comforted. I see a time of danger and defeat, and then a day of victory. I see this people, virtuous and free, founding a government on the rights of man. I see that government grown strong, that people prosperous, pushing its way across a continent. I see these villages become wealthy cities, these colonies great States, the Union we are about to found a power among the nations, and I know that future generations shall rise up and call us blessed.

Such might have been his thoughts as these founders of an empire sat for a while silent, face to face. It was the stillness of the last hour of night before the morning breaks; it was the quiet which precedes the storm. Suddenly, in some part of this hall a man rose up. His form was tall and angular, and his short wig

and coat of black gave him the appearance of a
clergyman. His complexion was swarthy, his nose
long and straight, his mouth large, but with a firm
expression on the thin lips, and his forehead exception-
ally high. The most remarkable feature of his face
was a pair of deep-set eyes, of piercing brilliancy,
changing so constantly with the emotions which they
expressed that none could tell the color of them. He
began to speak in a hesitating manner, faltering
through the opening sentences, as if fully convinced
of the inability, which he expressed, to do justice to
his theme. But presently, as he reviewed the wrongs
of the colonies through the past ten years, his cheek
glowed and his eye flashed fire and his voice rang out
rich and full, like a trumpet, through this hall. He
seemed not to speak like mortal man, thought one
who heard him ten years before in the Virginia House
of Burgesses; and a recent essayist in a leading
English Review has remarked, that, judging by effects,
he was one of the greatest orators that ever lived.*
There was no report made of his speech that day, but
from the notes which John Adams kept of the debate
we may learn what line of argument he took. He
spoke of the attacks made upon America by the king
and ministry of Great Britain, counselled a union
in the general defence, and predicted that future generations would quote the proceedings of this Congress
with applause. A step in advance of his time, as he
had ever been, he went far beyond the spirit of the
other delegates, who, with the exception of the

* *Essays*, by A. Hayward, Esq., Q. C., vol. iii.

Adamses and Gadsden, did not counsel or desire independence. "An entire new government must be founded," was his cry; "this is the first in a never-ending succession of Congresses," his prophecy. And gathering up, as it was the gift of his genius to do, the thought that was foremost in every mind about him, he spoke it in a single phrase: "British oppression has effaced the boundaries of the several colonies; I am not a Virginian, but an American."

My countrymen, we cannot exaggerate the debt we owe this man. The strength of his intellect, the fervor of his eloquence, the earnestness of his patriotism and the courage of his heart placed him in the front rank of those early patriots, and he stands among them the model of a more than Roman virtue. His eloquence was one of the chief forces of the American Revolution—as necessary to that great cause as the intelligence of Franklin, the will of Samuel Adams, the pen of Thomas Jefferson, or the sword of Washington. In such times of a nation's trial there is always one voice which speaks for all. It echoes the spirit of the age—proud or defiant, glad or mournful, now raised in triumph, now lifted up in lamentation. Greece stood on the Bema with Demosthenes; indignant Rome thundered against Catiline with the tongue of Cicero. The proud eloquence of Chatham rang out the triumphs of the English name, and France stood still to hear her Mirabeau. Ireland herself pleaded for liberty when Henry Grattan spoke, and the voice of Patrick Henry was the voice of America, struggling to be free!

Rest in peace, pure and patriotic heart! Thy work is finished and thy fame secure. Dead for three-quarters of a century, thou art still speaking to the sons of men. Through all descending time thy countrymen shall repeat thy glowing words, and, as the pages of their greatest bard kept strong the virtue of the Grecian youth, so from the grave shalt thou, who " spoke as Homer wrote,"* inspire in the hearts of men to be that love of liberty which filled thine own !

Great as were at first the differences of interest and opinion among the members of the Congress of 1774, there were none which their patriotic spirits could not reconcile. It was the salvation of the Americans that they had chosen for their counsellors men who believed, with Thomas Jefferson, that " the whole art of government consists in the art of being honest,"† and who were enthusiastic lovers of their country. No matter how strong had been their individual opinions, or how dear the separate interests involved, there seemed to these men no sacrifice too great to make for the common cause. As the debates progressed different views were reconciled and pet theories sacrificed to the general judgment. Day after day they became more united and confidence increased. " This," wrote John Adams on the 17th of September, " was one of the happiest days of my life. In Congress we had noble sentiments and manly eloquence. This day convinced me that America will support the Massachusetts or perish with her."‡ After a full and free

---

* *Memoir of Thomas Jefferson*, vol. i., p. 3.   † *Idem*, p. 115.
‡ *Journal of John Adams*, vol. ii., p. 380.

discussion, in which the subject was considered in all
its aspects, it was decided that each colony was entitled to a single vote.   By this means the integrity of
the provinces was preserved, and out of it grew the
theory, so familiar to us, of the sovereignty of the
State.   It was next agreed upon to rest the rights of
the colonies on a historical basis.   By this wise determination the appearance of a revolution was avoided,
while the fact remained the same.   Nor was there a
sudden break in the long chain of the nation's history;
the change was gradual, not abrupt.   The common
law of England, under the benign influence of which
the young colonies had grown up, remained un-
changed, and when, in less than two years, the Declaration of Independence created a new government,
the commonwealth quietly took the place of king.
The revolution was then complete; the struggle which
followed was merely to secure it: and the American
grew strong with the belief that it was his part to defend, not to attack—to preserve, not to destroy; and
that he was fighting over again on his own soil the
battle for civil liberty which his forefathers had won in
England more than a century before.   We cannot too
highly prize the wisdom which thus shaped the strug
gle.   Having decided these points, the Congress agreed
upon a declaration of rights.   First, then, they named
as natural rights the enjoyment of life, liberty and fortune.   They next claimed, as British subjects, to be
bound by no law to which they had not consented by
their chosen representatives (excepting such as might
be mutually agreed upon as necessary for the regula-

tion of trade). They denied to Parliament all power
of taxation, and vested the right of legislation in their
own Assemblies. The common law of England they
declared to be their birthright, including the rights of
a trial by a jury of the vicinage, of public meetings
and petition. They protested against the maintenance
in the colonies of standing armies without their full
consent, and against all legislation by councils depend-
ent on the Crown. Having thus proclaimed their
rights, they calmly enumerated the various acts which
had been passed in derogation of them. These were
eleven in number, passed in as many years—the Sugar
Act, the Stamp Act, the Tea Act, those which provided
for the quartering of the troops, for the supersedure
of the New York Legislature, for the trial in Great
Britain of offences committed in America, for the reg-
ulation of the government of Massachusetts, for the
shutting of the port of Boston, and the last straw,
known as the Quebec Bill.

Their next care was to suggest the remedy. On
the 18th of October they adopted the articles of
American Association, the signing of which (on the
20th) should be regarded as the commencement of
the American Union. By its provisions, to which they
individually and as a body solemnly agreed, they
pledged the colonies to an entire commercial non-
intercourse with Great Britain, Ireland, the West
Indies, and such North American provinces as did not
join the Association, until the acts of which America
complained were all repealed. In strong language
they denounced the slave-trade, and agreed to hold

non-intercourse with all who engaged therein. They urged upon their fellow-countrymen the duties of economy, frugality and the development of their own resources; directed the appointment of committees in every town and village to detect and punish all violators of the Association, and inform each other from time to time of the condition of affairs; and bound themselves, finally, to carry out the provisions of the Association by the sacred ties of "virtue, honor and love of country."

Having thus declared their rights, and their fixed determination to defend them, they sought to conciliate their English brethren. In one of the most remarkable state papers ever written they called upon the people of Great Britain in a firm but affectionate tone to consider the cause for which America was contending as one in which the inhabitants of the whole empire were concerned, adroitly reminding them that the power which threatened the liberties of its American might more easily destroy those of its English subjects. They rehearsed the history of their wrongs, and "demanded nothing but to be restored to the condition in which they were in 1763." Appealing at last to the justice of the British nation for a Parliament which should overthrow the "power of a wicked and corrupt ministry," they used these bold and noble words: "Permit us to be as free as yourselves, and we shall ever esteem a union with you to be our greatest glory and our greatest happiness; we shall ever be ready to contribute all in our power to the welfare of the empire; we shall consider your enemies as our enemies, your interests as our own. But if you are determined that your ministers shall sport wantonly with the rights of mankind—if neither the voice of justice, the dictates of the law, the principles of the constitution, nor the suggestions of humanity can restrain your hands from shedding blood in such an impious cause—we must then tell you that we will never submit to be hewers of wood or drawers of water for any ministry or nation in the world."

In an address to the people of Quebec they described the despotic tendency of the late change in their government effected by the Quebec Bill, which threatened to deprive them of the blessings to which they were entitled on becoming English subjects, naming particularly the rights of representation, of trial by jury, of liberty of person and *habeas corpus*, of the tenure of land by easy rents instead of oppressive services, and especially that right so essential "to the advancement of truth, science, art and morality," " to the diffusion of liberal sentiments " and " the promotion of union "—" the freedom of the press." " These are the rights," said they, " without which a people cannot be free and happy," and " which we are, with one mind, resolved never to resign but with our lives." In conclusion, they urged the Canadians to unite with their fellow-colonists below the St. Lawrence in the measures recommended for the common good. They also prepared letters to the people of St. John's, Nova Scotia, Georgia, and East and West Florida, who were not represented in this Congress, asking for their co-operation and support.

Nor was anything omitted by these men which could soften the hearts of their oppressors. Declining to petition Parliament, they had addressed themselves to the people, recognizing in them for the first time the sovereign power. They now decided to petition the king. In words both humble and respectful, they renewed their allegiance to his crown, detailed the injuries inflicted on them by his ministers, and besought his interference in their behalf. "We ask," they said, "but for peace, liberty and safety. We wish not a diminution of the prerogative, nor do we solicit the grant of any new right in our favor. Your royal authority over us and our connection with Great Britain we shall always carefully and zealously endeavor to support and maintain." Solemnly professing that their "counsels were influenced by no other motive than a dread of impending destruction," they earnestly besought their "Most Gracious Sovereign" "in the name of his faithful people in America," "for the honor of Almighty God," "for his own glory," "the interest of his family," and the good and welfare of his kingdom, to suffer not the most sacred "ties to be further violated" in the vain hope "of effects" which, even if secured, could "never compensate for the calamities through which they must be gained."

There remained now for the Congress but one thing to do—to render to its countrymen an account of its stewardship. In a long letter to their constituents the delegates gave a summary of their proceedings, of the difficulties they had encountered, the opinions they had formed, the policy they had agreed

to recommend, and, with a mournful prophecy of the
trials that were at hand, urged their fellow-countrymen
"to be in all respects prepared for every contingency."
Such were, in brief, the memorable state papers issued
by the First Continental Congress. And, terrible as
were the dangers which seemed to threaten them from
without, its members were to be subjected to a trial
from within. On the 28th of September, Joseph
Galloway of Pennsylvania submitted to the Congress
his famous plan.* A man of talent and address, at
one time high in the opinion and confidence of Franklin, he stood at the head of the Pennsylvania dele-
gation. The Speaker of the House of Assembly, he
had wielded great influence in the policy of the province. Cold, cautious and at heart a thorough royalist,
he determined, if possible, to nip the patriotic move-
ment in the bud. Seconded by Duane of New York,
he moved that the Congress should recommend the
establishment of a British and American government,
to consist of a President-General, appointed by the
king, and a Grand Council, to be chosen by the several Legislatures; that the Council should have co-
ordinate powers with the British House of Commons,
either body to originate a law, but the consent of both
to be necessary to its passage; the members of the
Council to be chosen for three years, the President-
General to hold office at the pleasure of the king.
Here, then, was an ingenious trap in the very path of
the infant nation. Some men, and good ones, too,

* *Vide* TUCKER'S *Hist.*, vol. i., p. 111. SABINE'S *American Loyalists*, vol. i.,
p. 309. JOHN ADAMS' *Works*, vol. ii., p. 389.

fell into it. The project was earnestly supported by
Duane. The younger Rutledge thought it "almost
perfect," and it met with the warm approbation of the
conservative Jay. But wiser men prevailed. The
Virginian and Massachusetts members opposed it
earnestly. Samuel Adams saw in it the doom of all
hope for liberty, and Henry condemned in every
aspect the proposal to substitute for "a corrupt House
of Commons" a "corruptible" legislature, and entrust
the power of taxation to a body not elected directly
by the people. His views were those of the majority,
and the dangerous proposition met with a prompt
defeat. The Suffolk county resolutions, adopted on
the 9th of September at Milton, Massachusetts, had
reached Philadelphia and the Congress on the 17th,
and awakened in every breast the warmest admiration and sympathy. Resolutions were unanimously
adopted expressing these feelings in earnest language,
recommending to their brethren of Suffolk county
"a perseverance in the same firm and temperate conduct," and urging upon the people of the other colonies the duty of contributing freely to the necessities
of the Bostonians. There now came a still more
touching appeal from Massachusetts. "The governor," it said, "was suffering the soldiery to treat both
town and country as declared enemies;" the course
of trade was stopped; the administration of law
obstructed; a state of anarchy prevailed. Filled with
the spirit which in olden times had led the Athenians
to leave their city to the foe and make their ships
their country, this gallant people promised to obey

should the Congress advise them to "quit their town;" but if it is judged, they added, that "by maintaining their ground they can better serve the public cause, they will not shrink from hardship and danger." *   Such an appeal as this could not have waited long for a worthy answer from the men of the First American Congress. The letter was received upon October 6th. Two days later the official journal contains these words: "Upon motion it was resolved that this Congress approve the opposition of the inhabitants of the Massachusetts Bay to the execution of the late acts of Parliament; and if the same shall be attempted to be carried into execution, all America ought to support them in their opposition." "This," says the historian, "is the measure which hardened George the Third to listen to no terms." †   In vain conciliation and kind words; in vain all assurances of affection and of loyalty. The men of Massachusetts are traitors to their king, and the Congress of all the colonies upholds them in rebellion. "Henceforth," says Bancroft, "conciliation became impossible."

Having thus asserted their rights to the enjoyment of life, liberty and fortune; their resistance to taxation without representation; their purpose to defend their ancient charters from assault; having denounced

---

* The spirit of this people is reflected in a letter from Boston printed in the *Pennsylvania Packet* for Oct. 10, 1774, describing a conversation which the writer had with a fisherman. "I said: 'Don't you think it time to submit, pay for the tea, and get the harbor opened?' 'Submit? No. It can never be time to become slaves. I have yet some pork and meal, and when they are gone I will eat clams; and after we have dug up all the clam-banks, if the Congress will not let us fight, I will retreat to the woods: I am always sure of acorns!'"

† BANCROFT's *Hist.*, vol. vii., p. 115.

4

the slave trade in language which startled the world, and recognized, for the first time in history, the People as the source of Authority ; having laid the firm foundations of a Union based upon Freedom and Equality, —the First Congress passed out of existence on the 26th of October, after a session of two and fifty days. Half a hundred men, born in a new country, bred amid trials and privations, chosen from every rank of life, untried in diplomacy, unskilled in letters, untrained in statecraft, called suddenly together in a troubled time to advise a hitherto divided people, they had shown a tact, a judgment, a self-command and a sincere love of country hardly to be found in the proudest annals of antiquity. And their countrymen were worthy of them. If the manner in which they had fulfilled their duties had been extraordinary, the spirit with which their counsels were received was still more remarkable. In every part of the country the recommendations of the Congress were obeyed as binding law. No despotic power in any period of history exercised over the minds and hearts of men a more complete control. The Articles of Association were signed by tens of thousands, the spirit of Union grew strong in every breast, and the Americans steadily prepared to meet the worst. The stirring influence of this example penetrated to the most distant lands. "The Congress," wrote Dr. Franklin from London in the following winter, "is in high favor here among the friends of liberty." *   "For a long time," cried the elo-

* *Letter to Charles Thomson*, 5th Feb., 1775 ; WATSON's *Annals of Philadelphia*, vol. i., p. 421.

quent Charles Botta, "no spectacle has been offered
to the attention of mankind of so powerful an interest
as this of the present American Congress."* "It is
impossible," says the Scotch writer, Grahame, "to read
of its transactions without the highest admiration."†
"There never was a body of delegates more faithful
to the interests of their constituents," was the opinion
of David Ramsay, the historian.‡ "From the moment
of their first debates," De Tocqueville says, "Europe
was moved."§ The judgment of John Adams declared them to be, "in point of abilities, virtues and
fortunes, the greatest men upon the continent."||
Charles Thomson, in the evening of his well-spent
life, pronounced them the purest and ablest patriots
he had ever known;¶ and, in the very face of king
and Parliament, the illustrious Chatham spoke of them
the well-known words: "I must avow and declare that
in all my reading of history—and it has been my fa-
vorite study; I have read Thucydides and admired the
master states of the world—that for solidity of reason-
ing, force of sagacity and wisdom of conclusion, under
such a complication of circumstances, no nation or
body of men can stand in preference to the General Congress assembled in Philadelphia."** Long
years have passed, and there have been many changes

---

* OTIS's *Botta*, vol. i., p. 128.

† *Hist. of the U. S.*, by JAMES GRAHAME, LL.D., vol. ii., p. 496.

‡ *Hist. of the American Revolution*, by DAVID RAMSAY, M. D., vol. i., p. 174.

§ *La Démocratie en Amérique*, by ALEXIS DE TOCQUEVILLE, vol. iii., p. 182.

|| *John Adams' Letters to his Wife*, vol. i., p. 21.

¶ *Field-Book of the Revolution*, by B. J. LOSSING, vol. ii., p. 60—note.

** *Speech in Favor of the Removal of Troops from Boston*, Jan. 20, 1775.

in the governments of men. The century which has
elapsed has been crowded with great events, but the
calm judgment of posterity has confirmed that opinion, and mankind has not ceased to admire the spectacle which was once enacted here. "But that you
may be more earnest in the defence of your country,"
cried the great Roman orator, speaking in a vision
with the tongue of Scipio, "know from me that a certain place in heaven is assigned to all who have preserved, or assisted, or improved their country, where
they are to enjoy an endless duration of happiness.
For there is nothing which takes place on earth more
acceptable to the Supreme Deity, who governs all this
world, than those councils and assemblies of men,
bound together by law, which are termed states: the
founders and preservers of these come from heaven,
and thither do they return."* The founders and preservers of this Union have vanished from the earth,
those true lovers of their country have long since
been consigned into her keeping, but their memory
clings around this place, and hath hallowed it for ever-
more. Here shall men come as to a sanctuary. Here
shall they gather with each returning anniversary, and
as the story of these lives falls from the lips of him
who shall then stand where I stand to-day, their souls
shall be stirred within them and their hearts be lifted
up, and none shall despair of the Republic while she
can find among her children the courage, the wisdom,
the eloquence, the self-sacrifice, the lofty patriotism

* CICERO, *De Re Publica*, lib. vi.: *Somnium Scipionis*, ⅔ iii.

and the spotless honor of those who assembled in this hall an hundred years ago.

The conditions of life are always changing, and the experience of the fathers is rarely the experience of the sons. The temptations which are trying us are not the temptations which beset their footsteps, nor the dangers which threaten our pathway the dangers which surrounded them. These men were few in number, we are many. They were poor, but we are rich. They were weak, but we are strong. What is it, countrymen, that we need to-day? Wealth? Behold it in your hands. Power? God hath given it you. Liberty? It is your birthright. Peace? It dwells amongst you. You have a government founded in the heart of men, built by the people for the common good. You have a land flowing with milk and honey; your homes are happy, your workshops busy, your barns are full. The school, the railway, the telegraph, the printing-press have welded you together into one. Descend those mines that honeycomb the hills. Behold that commerce whitening every sea! Stand by your gates and see that multitude pour through them from the corners of the earth, grafting the qualities of older stocks upon one stem, mingling the blood of many races in a common stream, and swelling the rich volume of our English speech with varied music from an hundred tongues. You have a long and glorious history, a past glittering with heroic deeds, an ancestry full of lofty and imperishable examples. You have passed through danger, endured privation, been acquainted with sorrow, been tried by suffering. You have journeyed in safety through the wilderness and crossed in triumph the Red Sea of civil strife, and the foot of Him who led you hath not faltered nor the light of His countenance been turned away! It is a question for us now, not of the founding of a new government, but of the preservation of one already old; not of the formation of an independent power, but of the purification of a nation's life; not of the conquest of a foreign foe, but of the subjection of ourselves. The capacity of man to rule himself is to be proven in the days to come—not by the greatness of his wealth, not by his valor in the field, not by the extent of his dominion, not by the splendor of his genius. The dangers of to-day come from within. The worship of self, the love of power, the lust for gold, the weakening of faith, the decay of public virtue, the lack of private worth,—these are the perils which threaten our future; these are the enemies we have to fear; these are the traitors which infest the camp; and the danger was far less when Catiline knocked with his army at the gates of Rome than when he sat smiling in the Senate-House. We see them daily face to face—in the walk of virtue, in the road to wealth, in the path to honor, on the way to happiness. There is no peace between them and our safety. Nor can we avoid them and turn back. It is not enough to rest upon the past. No man or nation can stand still. We must mount upward or go down. We must grow worse or better. It is the Eternal Law—we cannot change it. Nor are we only concerned in what we do. This government which our

ancestors have built has been "a refuge for the
oppressed of every race and clime," where they have
gathered for a century. The fugitive of earlier times
knew no such shelter among the homes of men.
Cold, naked, bleeding, there was no safety for him
save at the altars of imagined gods. I have seen one
of the most famous of those ancient sanctuaries. On
a bright day in spring-time I looked out over acres of
ruins. Beside me the blue sea plashed upon a beach
strewn with broken marble. That sacred floor,
polished with the penitential knees of centuries, was
half hidden with heaps of rubbish and giant weeds.
The fox had his den among the stones and the fowl of
the air her nest upon the capitals. No sound dis-
turbed them in their solitude, save sometimes the
tread of an adventurous stranger, or the stealthy foot-
fall of the wild beasts and wilder men that crept down
out of the surrounding hills under cover of the night.
The god had vanished, his seat was desolate, the
oracle was dumb. Far different was the temple which
our fathers builded, and "builded better than they
knew." The blood of martyrs was spilled on its
foundations, and a suffering people raised its walls with
prayer. Temple and fortress, it still stands, secure,
and the smile of Providence gilds plinth, architrave
and column. Greed is alone the Tarpeia that can
betray it, and vice the only Samson that can pull it
down. It is the Home of Liberty, as boundless as a
continent, "as broad and general as the casing air;" a
"temple not made with hands;" a sanctuary that shall
not fall, but stand on for ever, founded in eternal truth!

My countrymen, the moments are quickly passing, and we stand like some traveller upon a lofty crag that separates two boundless seas. The century that is closing is complete. "The past," said your great statesman, "is secure." It is finished, and beyond our reach. The hand of detraction cannot dim its glories nor the tears of repentance wipe away its stains. Its good and evil, its joy and sorrow, its truth and falsehood, its honor and its shame, we cannot touch. Sigh for them, blush for them, weep for them, if we will; we cannot change them now. We might have done so once, but we cannot now. The old century is dying, and they are to be buried with him; his history is finished, and they will stand upon its roll for ever.

The century that is opening is all our own. The years that lie before us are a virgin page. We can inscribe them as we will. The future of our country rests upon us—the happiness of posterity depends on us. The fate of humanity may be in our hands. That pleading voice, choked with the sobs of ages, which has so often spoken to deaf ears, is lifted up to us. It asks us to be brave, benevolent, consistent, true to the teachings of our history—proving "divine descent by worth divine." It asks us to be virtuous, building up public virtue upon private worth; seeking that righteousness which exalteth nations. It asks us to be patriotic—loving our country before all other things; her happiness our happiness, her honor ours, her fame our own. It asks us in the name of Justice, in the name of Charity, in the name of Freedom, in the name of God!

My countrymen, this anniversary has gone by for ever, and my task is done. While I have spoken the hour has passed from us; the hand has moved upon the dial, and the Old Century is dead. The American Union hath endured an hundred years. Here, on this threshold of the future, the voice of Humanity shall not plead to us in vain. There shall be darkness in the days to come; danger for our courage; temptation for our virtue; doubt for our faith; suffering for our fortitude. A thousand shall fall before us and tens of thousands at our right hand. The years shall pass beneath our feet, and century follow century in quick succession. The generations of men shall come and go; the greatness of yesterday shall be forgotten to-day, and the glories of this noon shall vanish before to-morrow's sun; but America shall not perish, but endure while the spirit of our fathers animates their sons!

Letters of regret for non-attendance were read.

From the President.

LONG BRANCH, N. J., Sept. 5, 1874.

John M. Ogden, Walter Allison and Richard K. Betts, Committee of the Carpenters' Company: Your invitation to me to attend the hundredth anniversary meeting of the Continental Congress in their hall on this day has, from accumulation of papers and letters during my recent visit East, escaped my attention until this moment.

Please excuse apparent neglect. It would have afforded me pleasure to attend your exercises on an occasion of so much interest. I hope they will be attended with all the interest such an occasion should naturally inspire.   U. S. GRANT.

From the Secretary of State.

Hon. Hamilton Fish, Secretary of State, writes:

GENTLEMEN: I regret that official engagements compel me to decline the invitation with which you have honored me to attend the celebration of the 5th of next month, by the Carpenters' Company of Philadelphia, of the one hundredth anniversary of the meeting of the Continental Congress. But, although I may not be personally present, you will have my sympathies and my good wishes for the success of your patriotic celebration.   Very truly yours,

HAMILTON FISH.

WASHINGTON, Aug. 29.

From the Secretary of War.

Hon. Wm. W. Belknap, Secretary of War, writes:

GENTLEMEN: I greatly regret that I am unable to comply with your very kind invitation for Saturday, September 5th.

Yours very respectfully,

WM. W. BELKNAP,
Secretary of War.

Governor Hartranft writes:

EXECUTIVE CHAMBER. HARRISBURG, Pennsylvania, Aug. 31, 1874.

Messrs. John M. Ogden, Walter Allison, Richard K. Betts, Committee, etc.—GENTLEMEN: I have the honor to acknowledge the receipt of your invitation, on behalf of the Carpenters' Company of Phila-delphia, to preside at the celebration of the One Hun-dredth Anniversary of the meeting of the Continental Congress in this Hall on Saturday, the 5th day of September, and beg leave to return my thanks for the courtesy.

I sincerely regret that an official engagement, made imperative by my relations to the military service of the State, will prevent my participation in this cele-bration of the Carpenters' Company—an occasion that promises to be full of interest, and that will recall the many and thrilling associations connected with the old Hall, within whose venerable walls were held the deliberations that prepared the way for the institutions and liberty we to-day enjoy.

Surrounded with stately structures of brick, stone and marble, in the midst of busy marts, noisy with the hum of trade, within sight of wharves crowded with shipping stands the quaint old Hall of the Carpenters' Company, simple and unpretentious in its architecture, but grand in the memories that cluster about it, and eloquent of the change wrought in the prosperity and wealth of the great city that now stretches its ample and magnificent proportions miles away from the plain little edifice in which the First Congress assembled. Amid the storm and forebodings that attended the first session of the Continental Congress in 1774, would the most sanguine of the patriots there assembled have for a moment conceived of the grandeur of a century's growth of the country whose foundations were then so wisely and securely laid? It is proper, therefore, as your card of invitation states, "to make this Centennial a fitting remembrance of the gratitude the nation of to-day owes to the patriots of 1774."

Renewing my regrets that another engagement will forbid my attendance, I again thank you for the graceful compliment paid me in requesting me to preside at your celebration, which I hope will prove alike pleasant and instructive.

Very respectfully,
Your obedient servant,
J. F. HARTRANFT.

LETTER OF REGRET.

Benson J. Lossing, the historian, concludes his letter thus:

. . . . I rejoice that you have renovated your building, and that henceforth it is to be devoted to the uses for which it was originally erected, and so preserved in the form it presented when the Congress assembled therein. It is a patriotic act for which you merit and will receive the cordial thanks of every true American.

With that Hall in possession, the Carpenters' Company of Philadelphia will ever be associated with the most sacred events in the history of our country.

There the measures were begun which led to Independence; therefore Carpenters' Hall and Independence Hall should hold an equal place in the affections and reverence of the American people, and all defenders of the rights of man.

With the expression of my sincere thanks for your courtesy, I am, gentlemen, your friend and fellow-citizen, BENSON J. LOSSING.

Letters of regret were read from Commodore George H. Preble; Hon. John A. Dix, Governor of New York; Hon. Joel Parker, Governor of New Jersey; Hon. Julius Converse, Governor of Vermont; John Wm. Wallace, President of the Historical Society of Pennsylvania; and many other distinguished citizens.

The following hymn, written for the occasion, led by De Witt Clinton Moore, was sung standing with great spirit by the whole audience.

CENTENNIAL JUBILEE.

BY DR. A. BEECHER BARNES.

(Sung at the close of the Oration. Tune—" Auld Lang Syne.")

The rolling hours of time have past,
And brought a hundred years;
We sing their requiem at last
Amid the world's loud cheers.

The chorus of the nation's chime
And tuneful anthems rise,
Like music of the spheres sublime,
And shake the echoing skies.

Here, where tolled out the despot's knell,
    And freedom had its birth,
Where Independence Hall and Bell
    Rang out o'er all the earth—

Welcome, thrice welcome, mighty throng,
    From every land and sea ;
Come, join the everlasting song
    Of freedom's jubilee.

God of our Fathers ! first and last
    Devout we worship Thee ;
From every stain of sin and crime,
    Oh come and make us free.

Then pure and strong our land will be,
    And glory from above
Shall crown our first Centennial
    And city of our love.

Come, nations, kindred, tribes ! and see
    Our freedom sealed in blood,
And celebrate our liberty—
    Freedom to worship God !

A vote of thanks was then tendered to H. Armitt Brown, for his eloquent and thrilling oration, with a request that he furnish a copy for publication. Also, the thanks of the meeting to the Chairman, Mr. Welsh. The meeting then adjourned.

The following are the resolutions to which the signatures of the members of Congress, as seen in the fac-simile, were attached.

" We do, for ourselves, and the inhabitants of the several colonies whom we represent, firmly agree and associate, under the sacred ties of virtue, honor and love of country, as follows :

"First. That from and after the first day of December next we will not import, into British-America, from Great-Britain or Ireland, any goods, wares or merchandise whatsoever, or from any other place, any such goods, wares or merchandise, as shall have been exported from Great-Britain or Ireland ; nor will we, after that day, import any East-India tea from any part of the world ; nor any molasses, syrups, panelas, coffee or pimento from the British plantations or from Dominica ; nor wines from Madeira or the Western Islands ; nor foreign indigo.

"Second. We will neither import nor purchase any slave imported after the first day of December next ; after which time we will wholly discontinue the slave trade, and will neither be concerned in it ourselves, nor will we hire our vessels nor sell our commodities or manufactures to those who are concerned in it.

"Third. As a non-consumption agreement, strictly adhered to, will be an effectual security for the observation of the non-importation, we, as above, solemnly agree and associate that from this 'day we will not purchase or use any tea imported on account of the East-India Company, or any on which a duty hath been or shall be paid ; and from and after the first day of March next, we will not purchase or use any East-India tea whatever ; nor will we, nor shall any person for or under us, purchase or use any of those goods, wares or merchandise we have agreed not to import, which we shall know, or have cause to suspect, were imported after the first day of December, except such as come under the rules and directions of the tenth article, hereafter mentioned.

"Fourth. The earnest desire we have not to injure our fellow-subjects in Great-Britain, Ireland or the West-Indies induces us to suspend a non-exportation until the tenth day of September, 1775 : at which time, if the said acts and parts of acts of the British Parliament hereinafter mentioned are not repealed, we will not directly or indirectly export any merchandise or commodity whatsoever to Great-Britain, Ireland or the West-Indies, except rice to Europe.

"Fifth. Such as are merchants, and use the British and Irish trade, will give orders, as soon as possible, to their factors, agents and correspondents, in Great-Britain and Ireland, not to ship any goods to them on any pretence whatsoever, as they cannot be received in America; and if any merchant, residing in Great-Britain or Ireland, shall directly or indirectly ship any goods, wares or merchandise for America, in order to break the said non-importation agreement, or in any manner contravene the same, on such unworthy conduct being well attested, it ought to be made public; and, on the same being so done, we will not, from thenceforth, have any commercial connection with such merchant.

"Sixth. That such as are owners of vessels will give positive orders to their captains, or masters, not to receive on board their vessels any goods prohibited by the said non-importation agreement, on pain of immediate dismission from their service.

"Seventh. We will use our utmost endeavors to improve the breed of sheep, and increase their number to the greatest extent; and to that end, we will kill them as seldom as may be, especially those of the most profitable kind, nor will we export any to the West-Indies or elsewhere; and those of us, who are or may become overstocked with or can conveniently spare any sheep, will dispose of them to our neighbors, especially to the poorer sort, on moderate terms.

"Eighth. We will, in our several stations, encourage frugality, economy, and industry, and promote agriculture, arts and the manufactures of this country, especially that of wool; and will discountenance and discourage every species of extravagance and dissipation, especially all horse-racing, and all kinds of gaming, cock-fighting, exhibitions of shows, plays, and other expensive diversions and entertainments; and on the death of any relation or friend, none of us, or any of our families, will go into any further mourning-dress than a black crape or ribbon on the arm or hat for gentlemen, and a black ribbon and necklace for ladies, and we will discontinue the giving of gloves and scarfs at funerals.

"Ninth. Such as are vendors of goods or merchandise will not take advantage of the scarcity of goods, that may be occasioned by this association, but will sell the same at the rates we have been respectively accustomed to do for twelve months last past. And if any vendor of goods or merchandise shall sell any such goods on higher terms, or shall, in any manner, or by any device whatsoever, violate or depart from this agreement, no person ought, nor will any of us, deal with any such person, or his or her factor or agent, at any time thereafter, for any commodity whatever.

"Tenth. In case any merchant, trader or other person shall import any goods or merchandise after the first day of December and before the first day of February next, the same ought forthwith, at the election of the owner, to be either reshipped or delivered up to the committee of the county or town wherein they shall be imported, to be stored at the risk of the importer until the non-importation agreement shall cease, or be sold under the direction of the committee aforesaid ; and in the last-mentioned case, the owner or owners of such goods shall be reimbursed out of the sales the first cost and charges, the profit, if any, to be applied toward relieving and employing such poor inhabitants of the town of Boston as are immediate sufferers by the Boston Port Bill ; and a particular account of all goods so returned, stored or sold to be inserted in the public papers ; and if any goods or merchandises shall be imported after the said first day of February, the same ought forthwith to be sent back again, without breaking any of the packages thereof.

"Eleventh. That a committee be chosen in every county, city and town, by those who are qualified to vote for representatives in the legislature, whose business it shall be attentively to observe the conduct of all persons touching this association ; and when it shall be made to appear, to the satisfaction of a majority of any such committee, that any person within the limits of their appointment has violated this association, that such majority do forthwith cause the truth of the case to be published in the gazette ; to the end, that all such foes to the rights of British-America may be publicly known and universally contemned as the enemies of American liberty ; and thenceforth we respectively will break off all dealings with him or her.

"Twelfth. That the committee of correspondence, in the respective colonies, do frequently inspect the entries of their custom-

5

houses, and inform each other, from time to time, of the true state thereof, and of every other material circumstance that may occur relative to this association.

"Thirteenth. That all manufactures of this country be sold at reasonable prices, so that no undue advantage be taken of a future scarcity of goods.

"Fourteenth. And we do further agree and resolve that we will have no trade, commerce, dealings or intercourse whatsoever, with any colony or province, in North-America, which shall not accede to or which shall hereafter violate this association, but will hold them as unworthy of the rights of freemen, and as inimical to the liberties of their country.

"And we do solemnly bind ourselves and our constituents, under the ties aforesaid, to adhere to this association, until such parts of the several acts of Parliament, passed since the close of the last war, as impose or continue duties on tea, wine, molasses, syrups, pancles, coffee, sugar, pimento, indigo, foreign paper, glass and painters' colors, imported into America, and extend the powers of the admiralty courts beyond their ancient limits, deprive the American subject of trial by jury, authorize the judge's certificate to indemnify the prosecutor from damages, that he might otherwise be liable to, from a trial by his peers, require oppressive security from a claimant of ships or goods seized, before he shall be allowed to defend his property, are repealed. And until that part of the act of the 12 G. 3, ch. 24, entitled 'An act for the better securing His Majesty's dock-yards, magazines, ships, ammunition and stores,' by which any persons charged with committing any of the offences therein described, in America, may be tried in any shire or county within the realm, is repealed ; and until the four acts, passed the last session of Parliament—viz., that for stopping the port and blocking up the harbor of Boston, that for altering the charter and government of the Massachusetts Bay, and that which is entitled 'An act for the better administration of justice, etc." and that ' For extending the limits of Quebec, etc.'—are repealed. And we recommend it to the provincial conventions, and to the committees in the respective colonies, to establish such further regulations as they may think proper, for carrying into execution this association.

"The foregoing association, being determined upon by the Congress, was ordered to be subscribed by the several members thereof; and thereupon we have hereunto set our respective names accordingly.

"*In Congress, Philadelphia, October* 20, 1774.

      "Signed,   PEYTON RANDOLPH, *President.*

New Hampshire,
{
John Sullivan,
Nathaniel Folsom.

Massachusetts Bay,
{
Thomas Cushing,
Samuel Adams,
John Adams,
Robert Treat Paine.

Rhode Island,
{
Stephen Hopkins,
Samuel Ward.

Connecticut,
{
Eliphalet Dyer,
Roger Sherman,
Silas Deane.

New York,
{
Isaac Low,
John Alsop,
John Jay,
James Duane,
William Floyd,
Henry Wisner,
S. Boerum,
Philip Livingston.

New Jersey,
{
James Kinsey,
William Livingston,
Stephen Crane,
Richard Smith,
John De Hart.

Pennsylvania,	Joseph Galloway, John Dickinson, Charles Humphreys, Thomas Mifflin, Edward Biddle, John Morton, George Ross.
New Castle, etc.,	Cæsar Rodney, Thomas M'Kean, George Read.
Maryland,	Matthew Tilghman, Thomas Johnson, William Paca, Samuel Chase.
Virginia,	Richard Henry Lee, George Washington, P. Henry, Jun., Richard Bland, Benjamin Harrison, Edmund Pendleton.
North Carolina,	William Hooper, Joseph Hewes, R. Caswell.
South Carolina,	Henry Middleton, Thomas Lynch, Christopher Gadsden, John Rutledge, Edward Rutledge.''

www.ingramcontent.com/pod-product-compliance
Lightning Source LLC
Chambersburg PA
CBHW021513090426
42739CB00007B/591